The Forgotten Art of Happiness

The Forgotten Art of Happiness

Ali Zakaria

Published by Ali Zakaria, 2018.

THE FORGOTTEN ART OF HAPPINESS

First edition. September 22, 2018.

Copyright © 2018 Ali Zakaria.

ISBN: 978-1393914891

Written by Ali Zakaria.

Table of Contents

The Forgotten Art of Happiness

52 Ideas That Will Change Your Life

ALI ZAKARIA

2018

First edition, 2018
ISBN 13: 978-1724560629
ISBN 10: 172456062X
www.alizakaria.com[1]

Acknowledgments

I would love to thank you, the reader, as you made the decision to take a step closer to your happiness and buy this book.

I would love to thank my mother and sister, as they encouraged me to finish this book.

I would love to thank myself for finishing this book.

I would love to thank the persons that agreed to be interviewed for this book.

I would love to thank Amber Richberger, my editor; it is because of her this book looks so good.

I would love to thank the Actions for Happiness movement in the United Kingdom, as they provided me with powerful resources.

I would love to thank Brené Brown, as she is tackling a new topic that changed the way I look at happiness.

I would love to thank my job, as it provided me with time and money while writing this book.

I would love to thank every person that I had a conversation with about this book; you all have really inspired me.

I would love to thank every person who told me that I would not finish this book; it is because of you I have finished it.

"Ali Zakaria provides advice that is both simple and wise, both rigorous and practical. Read the book, apply its lessons, and enjoy higher levels of fulfillment and happiness"
Tal Ben-Shahar
Best-selling author of Happier: Learn the Secrets to Daily Joy and Lasting Fulfillment and lecturer on positive psychology at Harvard University.

Preface

S

ince my second year in law school, I felt there was more to life and that I could live a life that was happier and more fulfilling. I started to attend seminars and workshops, read books, and I even tried to build a business. I was employed as a judge in 2009 but always felt that it wasn't my true calling. Even if some people see it as a very prestigious position and believe I should be grateful for having such an opportunity, I always felt that there was more. After spending so many years studying positive psychology, human behavior, awareness and consciousness, and getting certified in neuro-linguistic programming (NLP) and Time Line Therapy (TLT), I felt that I had a message to share. I feel that if everyone knew what I knew, they would live a happier life and the world would be a better place.

I thought about writing a book, but I was not confident because I had never written before. It took me four years to hear the following quote from the fellow writer Louisa May Alcott: "Don't worry too much about your process."[1] After that, I began writing, telling myself I would enjoy the writing process; I would worry about publishing later. After two and a half years, I finished my book without even noticing. I was just researching, experimenting, writing, and interviewing and I enjoyed every single moment of it.

Table of Contents

Part Three: Happy Body

Part Four: Happy Relationships

Citations

Foreword
by Eric Edmeades

I was not happy, and neither was my wife. Life was testing us and we were failing.

We had invested in a movie studio and found, shortly after investing and taking control of the company, that the owners had defrauded us. They had misrepresented almost everything about the company and then, to make matters worse, one of them stole the technology we had purchased and set up a competitive company with the same name.

Soon it turned out that they had been using the company to raise funds for scam after scam and we inherited all the difficulties that came with their behavior; within a few weeks of purchasing the company, I was slammed with a variety of legal threats and lawsuits. Then I found out that one of the partners had done the transaction under a false name and had, previously, faced prosecution that carried a 493-year jail sentence had they not allowed him a soft plea-bargain.

Every week, we lived in fear. Every week, we worried about making payroll and preserving everyone's jobs. Every week, we worried about our own future. Every week, we were stressed, worried, and unhappy.

My wife and I went for a walk and talked about our unhappiness and our stress. We reached a decision; happiness was up to us. We realized that there were people with far less than us that still found happiness. And so we decided to be happy. No matter what. Not every minute of every day, but as a habit. So, we created happiness rituals.

After a few days, we felt a lot better. Things were still scary but we decided that most of our unhappiness was about the unknown. Like the coward that dies a thousand deaths, we were unhappy because of what might or might not happen.

We found happiness. Genuine happiness. Some of the people around us thought we had finally snapped under the pressure, but it was exactly the opposite; we no longer gave in to the pressure and spent time doing things that we enjoyed.

Over the next few weeks, a number of nearly miraculous things happened. Neill Blomkamp, the famed South African director of District 9, approached our company looking for a major special effects sequence for his upcoming film Elysium. Next came requests to work on Pirates of the Caribbean III and Iron Man II.

My more esoteric friends suggested that we won all these contracts because we had changed our attitude, that our positive thinking had helped us attract these opportunities.

Okay. Could be.

What I do know, however, is this: Had we failed to find happiness until our circumstances changed, we may well have won those contracts and then found happiness, perpetuating the idea that happiness is created by external events.

Instead, we found happiness irrespective of external events and the lessons learned in doing so have been invaluable to us. I am ever grateful that we found happiness before our fortunes changed.

Today, I see people searching. Searching for meaning. Searching for their life's purpose. And I wonder.

I wonder if, perhaps, the only real purpose of one's life is to enjoy it.

Many years ago, I developed my own definition of success. For me, success in a person's life is most easily measured by the number of days they are truly happy. So far, I have not found a better definition. And, with that in mind, I have given a great deal of thought to what happiness is and how various people achieve it.

When Ali contacted me from Egypt and asked me to write a foreword for his book on happiness, I was only too eager to oblige. Happiness, I believe, is one of the most important topics of discussion at the moment; when people are unhappy, they do terrible things to themselves and to others.

I was also intrigued by Ali's perspective; he has spent almost ten years collectively as a judge in the Ministry of Justice in Egypt and as a public prosecutor. This tells me that Ali has seen a great many people that were far from happy.

The absence of happiness is, frankly, a major social and economic problem all over the world. People are less productive when they are unhappy. Further down the scale, unhappy people turn to excessive television, non-productive foods, abuse of alcohol and drugs, and, in extreme cases, suicide. The Centers for Disease Control in the United States reports that rates of suicide in the US have increased by 25% over the last twenty years. Many states have seen suicide rates soar by 30% and even 40% during the same period.

To put this in proper perspective, consider that the average American is twice as likely to die from suicide than from homicide. Furthermore, Americans are 300 times more likely to die from suicide than from terrorism. 300 times.

Here we are in the safest time in history and record numbers of people are opting out.

Why?

There are many reasons but one way to look at it is that, quite simply, those people were no longer happy.

This book is not some lightweight personal development book about happiness, it is a down-to-earth and practical guide to happiness that includes specific tactics and strategies to help you improve your overall happiness by, for instance, removing things that are blocking your happiness, understanding how your health and fitness plays a role, and giving you specific strategies for incremental emotional improvements.

Finally, the interviews are excellent.

In Part Five, Ali has included a number of interviews with people who participated in the 100 Happy Days Challenge and the insights are fascinating.

It is easy to recommend a book by telling people that they will be happy because they read it, but it is not every day that I can recommend a book and tell you that you will be happier because you read it.

Sincerely,

Eric Edmeades

Introduction

I was very worried about writing this book but there was always a voice inside my head saying every human being has his own experience in life. I knew sharing these experiences would enhance other people's experiences and would prevent them from making the same mistakes. I believe that everyone should share his experience with the world. The medium through which the experience is shared is not important. It can be shared by writing a book, hosting a seminar, attending a support group, creating a YouTube channel, or even launching a blog.

I was always searching for methods, theories, and activities so I could live a better life, so I could feel good. At the same time, I am quite a lazy person (it took me four years to start writing this book and I wrote it in only two and a half years). Consequentially, I was searching for easy ways to live happier and more contently. There is a famous book called *The Secret* which served as my first introduction to the power of thoughts. I learned from this book that changing your thoughts and ideas can change your state and mood instantly and that our ideas shape our lives. Here is an example: In a football match, when one team scores a goal, half the audience gets very excited and happy and the other half becomes sad. Although they are both looking at the same event, it is not the event that matters but rather their perspective. By changing your thoughts about the things that happen in your life, you can become happy, miserable, motivated, or discouraged. This is something that does not take too much effort; it only requires knowledge, awareness, and consciousness.

After three years of watching videos, reading articles, attending seminars, experimenting with ideas and theories, and interviewing many people, like nutritionists and coaches, I discovered that changing your thoughts is very helpful in achieving what you want. However, it is not enough. This is why the title of this book is *The Forgotten Art of Happiness: 52 Ideas That Will Change Your Life*. Living a happier life requires maintaining a strong mindset and following daily routines and actions. Much like when we go to the gym so we can have a good-looking body, we need to make changes in order to become happier people.

I wanted the ideas of this book to be genuine and real, so I promised myself I would apply every idea before including it. When an idea made me experience a positive feeling, I wrote it down. When it did not, I did not write it down. All the ideas in this book are tested either by me or by me and a few others. In addition, I promised myself that every idea would be as practical as possible because I suffered a lot from people who told me to think positively and, when asked how, responded by saying, "Just think positive." If you struggle with practicing any of these ideas, please contact me through alizakaria@me.com and we will figure it out together.

The Structure of the Book:

THIS BOOK IS DIVIDED into five parts: Happy Mind, Happy Actions, Happy Body, Happy Relationships, and Interviews. Each part contains ideas and each idea contains instructions, examples, and exercises that will help you apply such ideas to your life.

I have chosen to arrange these parts in a specific order, starting with the easiest and ending with the most challenging. In the first part, you can change your mindset instantly by gaining knowledge and awareness. In the following two parts you must depend on yourself to apply the ideas; you neither need the help nor the interference of anyone else. Finally, by applying the ideas of the first three parts, you will have the ability and the confidence to apply the ideas of the fourth part.

My journey followed these same steps. After having my mindset changed and my mind filled with valuable information, I began to take actions toward achieving my dreams. I started taking care of my body, which resulted in building some self-credibility. I found inner peace and everlasting happiness. Only then did I start to have healthy relationships; as I no longer relied on the approval of others, I started to keep the relationships that encouraged my new, happy life and got rid of those that took away my inner peace and happiness.

This book may broaden your mind and inspire you to find and create your own happiness. You may form your own ideas and methods that work better for you, and that's the goal. You know yourself better than I possibly could. Use this book as a tool to find *your* inner peace and *your* everlasting happiness.

How to Deal with This Book?

YOU CAN CHOOSE TO APPLY this book's ideas in any way you wish. However, I am going to provide you with two methods that may help. The first approach is to apply one idea per week so you can have 52 weeks, or a year, of happiness. If you find yourself not committing to the idea you choose, you might want to find a partner who wants to apply the same idea as you. You can easily find such a partner through our community on Facebook (A Year of Happiness). You can also read it all at once and whichever ideas suit you will sink in and you will apply them unconsciously.

What is Happiness?

ACCORDING TO MERRIAM-Webster's Online Dictionary, happiness is a state of well-being and contentment.[2] However, Max Strom describes it as the daily experience of a meaningful life.[3] My definition of happiness, however, is the continuous experience of positive feelings. This is why people confuse happiness with other positive feelings; they say they are happy when they are proud, hopeful, inspired, grateful, or experiencing any other positive feeling. I believe that happiness is finding satisfaction in what life offers you and what you offer life. Earning happiness is like eating to take care of your body. You can not only drink water or eat one type of food; it is the combination of many kinds of food and beverages that bring health to your body. It is the same when it comes to happiness; it is a combination of different activities and mindsets that you do or stop doing that brings happiness to your life.

There are two types of things that bring happiness to your life. The first includes common events, things, and activities that bring happiness to the majority of human beings, and we are going to discover those things later in this book. The second type of things are the unique things that bring happiness to one specific person and those things differ from one person to another. Later on, we will go over some exercises that will help you discover those things.

Have You Ever Asked Yourself, "Why Should I Be Happy"?

I KNOW IT MIGHT SEEM like a stupid question but what I want to emphasize is why we have to take happiness seriously. There are countless benefits of being happy and we are going to find out some of them together. One of the benefits of being happy is that our brains function much better when we are happy. There was an experiment facilitated by psychologists. They divided a group of people into two groups: the happy group and neutral group. Then they gave both groups the same task. Results showed that only 13% of the neutral group managed to finish the task in ten minutes, while 75% of the happy group managed to finish it in the same amount of time. This practical experiment shows that our brains tend to be more productive when we are happy.

Another benefit of being happy is that happiness makes us healthier. It is a cliché that laughter is the best medicine but it has been scientifically proven that laughter lowers the risk of having a heart attack by 50% by lowering blood pressure, one of the major causes of heart diseases. A study conducted in Harvard by Laura Kubzansky[4] showed that having attributes such as enthusiasm or optimism and having a supportive group of family or friends tends to help people avoid many diseases, such as heart attack, stroke, diabetes, and depression. This study made me believe we should take the concept of a happier life seriously and stop seeing it as a luxury.

Part One:
Happy Mind

"M

y mind." This was the answer I received when I asked Anna from Croatia about an obstacle she had to overcome to be happy. In this part, we will share some principles and philosophies that will help you bring happiness into your life.

Your mindset is the foundation of your happiness; if you are applying the teachings of this book without having the right mindset, it will not work. At the same time, finding the right mindset is the easiest part of the happiness journey because you can do it by yourself anywhere and anytime.

1. Decide

THE FIRST THING YOU have to do in order to be happy is decide to be happy. I always made decisions I did not stick with but after a while I discovered the decision was not something that you make once and for all; it is something you need to renew as long as you walk through life. To exemplify, when you subscribe to a gym and work out every day, you have decided that going to the gym is important to you. You don't think about that decision again, about whether it was right or wrong, whenever you have a muscle strain; you may take some rest, but you never give up.

Happiness is the same; you should know that happiness is something you have to decide, create, and experience in your daily life. Most of us face a similar problem after we make the decision to be happy. We negotiate with ourselves along the way, we doubt our decisions, and we question ourselves. *Why should we be happy when everyone is neutral? Why should we be happy when we are faced with so many challenges in life?* You should know that the middle of the road is not the place to make up your mind or make a decision that you should have made sooner. You should also be aware of the reason why you are reconsidering the decision; it might be due to hunger, fatigue, stress, or even hanging out with the wrong people.

You are in control. Knowing you are in control of your life empowers you to be the cause, not the effect, of your circumstances and to be proactive, to change what you don't want or don't like. Whenever you say "I am not happy" because of an external factor's effect, you are actually saying that this factor is bigger and stronger than you, which is not true. If you notice the things you can control, you will realize they are way more than any constant in life. When you focus on the constants that can't be changed and try to control them, you feel paralyzed.

When you begin to do what you want, no matter how small it is, you gradually gain control over the bigger things in your life. Neglect any external factor that may force you to do something you don't want to do or may stop you from doing something that you want.

Sonya, a woman from California, said the following when describing why she chose to pursue a more happy life. "When I was about twenty-two years old, I realized the weight of anger is too heavy. Happiness and gratitude affect my body more positively than lower frequency emotions. I have watched people in my life live in a constant state of sadness, seeing the world through the eyes of pain, and I realized that is not the kind of life I want to live. I chose to see life through the eyes of gratitude instead."

Deciding to be happy is commanding your mind to focus only on the events that make you happy and neglect all others. Scientists estimate that our brain receives 400 billion bits of information per second, but the conscious mind processes only 2000 bits of them.[5] The 2000 bits of information that the conscious mind processes and focuses on are the result of our decisions and previous experiences. Accordingly, this means we can choose the things we focus on, only if we decide so, but we have to be consciously aware of what we are focusing on until it becomes a habit.

Here is an exercise that you can try. Look around you, wherever you are, and search for things that are red. Now close your eyes and try to remember something around you that is a different color; you will notice you can only remember the red things. This exercise shows that we can command our mind to focus on specific things; the problem is that we are used to focusing on the negative things and it becomes a habit. By saying you are used to complaining because you started when you were young, your mind will only focus on the things that it can complain about. You have to rewire your brain to focus on other things; you have to consciously switch your attention to the positive things until it becomes a habit.

2. Clean Your Mind

WE HAVE ALL EXPERIENCED tough situations that have turned into bad memories and, due to overthinking them, kept coming back again and again. On a regular basis, we should clean these bad memories from our minds in order to live happily. But how? First, you have to accept your pitfalls and mistakes; you have to acknowledge that those mistakes were necessary at the moment you made them because they made you the person you are now. Second, you have to monitor your thoughts. Whenever a bad memory comes to your mind, neglect it and replace it with something that can boost your mood. You can call a friend or read something useful; it could be anything intended to break the pattern or the loop of thinking about the negative memory. When you hold onto negative memories, you're blocking the energy of the universe from flowing through you and preventing yourself from doing whatever you want. In the beginning it will be quite challenging and you may lose focus and drown in those bad memories but, if you persist, your bad memories will no longer have control over you.

Live in the present, neither in the past nor in the future. The past will only bring you regret and shame and the future will only bring you anxiety. This does not mean you should never think about your future or your past, but the magic formula is to think about it as long as it is empowering you. Think of the past to learn from it and think of the future to be prepared for it.

The famous book *The Power of Now* by Eckhart Tolle contains valuable information about how to live in the present. The book taught me a lot about life. It taught me there was always a dimension of life in front of me, but I was not living in it at all; I was always living in either the fantasy of the future or the regret and shame of the past. Since I discovered the dimension of the present moment, I discovered that the memories that felt very real were only a thought in my head and that I could focus on the present, which is more realistic than any other thought in my head.

We should neither think about the future nor the past unless it's bringing joy to the present by reminding us of an achievement or a funny situation or if thinking about the future would bring us hope. Otherwise, we should be living in the present because it'll never come again. The present is more valuable and important than the past or the future; it's a gift. We must live it before it passes away so that we do not ruin the moment by thinking of the past or the future that may bring us sorrow or fear. The future seems scary but, when it comes, it won't be as scary as it seemed before.

3. You Are Ready for It

THE THING YOU BELIEVE you need in order to get where you want to go is often standing in your way. In other words, the qualifications we think are required to do anything we want are actually the only obstacles preventing us from doing them. If we allow ourselves to listen to our hearts more often and believe that we have all it takes to do what we want, our potential is going to be limitless. If we only knew that the thing holding us back was that story we kept telling ourselves, that imaginary obstacle that says we are not qualified or worthy enough is not real. For example, if you are a recruiter and want to hire a new employee and there are two candidates who applied who have the same technical skills, you will be more inclined to hire the one who projects an image of confidence and ambition in the way he talks, the way he walks, and the way he answers questions. He is certain he can fulfill the job description while the other one hesitates and is nervous.

To illustrate, what if we apply these examples to our lives, whether in our jobs or in our relationships, leaving the control for negative feelings, like the feeling of worthlessness or being unprepared; we always get these feelings when we have a calling to do something. Those feelings are the only barrier; they are the only thing making us feel unprepared. Imagine a child who wants to learn how to ride a bicycle but always refuses to try. He will never be ready unless he tries; he may fall, but eventually he will learn.

4. Forgive Yourself

WHENEVER YOU MAKE MISTAKES, do not be harsh on yourself. It is not going to help you; we are all human beings and everybody makes mistakes. In the Islamic religion, there is a hadith (a quote by the prophet Muhammad PBUH) which states that God loves people who seek forgiveness; he even prefers forgiveness seekers over people who don't sin at all and will certainly forgive anyone who seeks his forgiveness. Sometimes we forget that we are meant to make mistakes. This is why God made forgiveness. Then we created phrases like: "I'm sorry" and "I apologize." We invented the eraser; if there was no need for them, we wouldn't have created them in the first place.

Sometimes we idealize the way we should behave, neglecting our human nature. However, you may not use this concept as an excuse to make mistakes. Instead, use it as a way to comfort yourself and to overcome the despair you might feel after making mistakes. Let it be a way to overcome the hopelessness that comes after making mistakes, not an excuse to commit them.

Imagine how you would treat a close friend who came to you with the feeling of guilt after doing something wrong. Which words would you choose to say and which tone of voice would you be using? Just take a moment and imagine that. Now imagine how you would treat yourself when you feel guilty for doing something wrong. You might notice that it is quite different. Research has shown that 76% of people are more compassionate to others than they are to themselves and only 6% are more compassionate to themselves. So next time you feel you have done something wrong and you regret it, try to be your ally rather than your enemy and treat yourself as you are your closest friend because you really are. Dr. Kristin Neff, a self-compassion expert, has talked about self-compassion and how it is really connected to one's well-being. She said that "self-compassionate people tend to be healthier and happier".[6] It's not about being easy on ourselves; it is about getting out of our own way.

5. Happiness Requires Some Sadness

TAL BEN-SHAHAR ONCE said that it is inhuman and unrealistic to be happy all the time and that people who are considered happy are only happy most of the time. I believe we are in the age of comfort; everything has an app, from ordering food to laundry, and even this book may have been purchased from an online store. We used to be at ease most of the time, which is not a bad thing, but life just doesn't work this way. Sometimes life is uncomfortable. We may go through hell from time to time, but this is something we should experience so we can appreciate the blessing of a peaceful day when it comes. Although some situations may be hard, at the end of the day these situations build character. Think about how the universe is made of duality: morning and night, big and small, tall and short, men and women. Imagine a world without morning or a world without men. This world would be ridiculous and boring. Everything in life was made in pairs; this also applies to sadness and happiness. We have to experience the feeling of sadness so we can appreciate and recognize happiness.

I wanted to learn more about the experiences of others, so I reached out to people around the world and asked them about their journey to happiness. Lily, a woman from Mexico City, said the following when asked about when she decided to seek happiness.

"After a bad break up, I was so depressed that my health was affected. Doctors tried to find the source of my illness. They thought it was thyroid cancer but it turned out to be the effects of a profound depression. I decided to take control of my life and go to therapy."

Much like Lily, Anna from Croatia faced health issues and stagnation due to her unhappiness. Anna told me the following: "I was diagnosed with a panic attack disorder, depression, and anxiety when I was nineteen years old. I became an introvert. This struggle went on for years. I lost many friends and failed a year of college. One of the first things I had to do was move my focus from big things and focus on small victories. I had to stop pitying myself, forgive myself, and forgive others."

When I asked Anna from Munich a similar question, she noted more common dissatisfactions. "I was really unhappy with my last job," she told me. "I had conflicts with my boss and I felt totally uneasy and uncomfortable. At one point I noticed that it affected my whole life. I got sadder and sadder. I lost the love of my life. I felt I was more depressed than before. I was so worn out after work that I didn't want to do sports or meet friends anymore because it was exhausting. That was when I noticed I needed to change and become a 'happy' person again."

Krista from St. Louis also noted fulfillment issues in the workplace. "Getting fired and getting divorced initially made me sad and depressed. I thought the world was working against me but I quickly realized the opposite was true. These instances cleared my path so I could become the woman I am now."

One of the most influential stories I heard came from a Californian woman named Sonya. She told me she grew up in a family with a lot of violence and alcohol abuse. As a kid, many people told her she would not amount to anything. She chose to live a life vastly different from the one everyone assumed she would live. She vowed to stay true to herself.

Finally, Darine and Sandra from Egypt had comparable responses and I was beginning to see a trend. Darine told me being sad was actually taking its toll on her relationships with most of the people that she loved and cared about. Sandra, like Darine, seemed to suffer from a similar outlook. "I decided to be happy when I realized I was sad and unsatisfied most of the time," Sandra told me. "My decision can be attributed to the job I didn't like and a certain group of people who weren't good for me."

After interviewing so many people who considered themselves happy, I realized a lot of them had to go through tragedy before they could lead happier lives. Sometimes the most tragic situations in our lives can lead us to the life we always wanted.

There will be times in life where things may not make us feel an immediate happiness, but they will make us feel happy later or maybe after we die, when we can see all the good deeds that we have done. For example, all the things you are putting aside right now, which you think will not make you happy, will actually do the contrary; they are the seeds you plant now so you can reap their benefits in the future. They are small things that might not make us happy instantly but they will make us happy eventually. The Dalai Lama, a spiritual leader of the Tibetan people, once said it doesn't matter when it makes you happy; what matters is how long the happiness lasts.

6. Accept Your Negative Feelings

THERE ARE TWO KINDS of people that don't experience negative feelings: psychopaths and dead people. So, if you are having some negative feelings, congratulations; you are a sane, living human being. Knowing you don't have to be happy all the time makes you accept the fact there will be times you will feel bad. This is how you distinguish the feeling of happiness, value it, and enjoy it. It is like gravity. We don't complain about being confined to Earth because it is beyond our control; on the contrary, we complain about things we can change. You just accept the fact that you were, are, and will always be attached to the earth. Being aware that you are not meant to be happy all the time takes the stress away, no matter what is happening around you.

Tal Ben-Shahar, a leading lecturer in positive psychology, once said that "the level of depression in our modern world has increased because people refuse to feel bad. They expect to feel good all the time and this expectation makes them stressed and frightened whenever they feel that they are not happy."[7] What we do not realize is that we might have those negative feelings but we can choose to act and behave in a way that will make those feelings go away. The problem is not that we feel oppressed, offended, or any other negative feeling; the problem is that we are refusing to feel that way. If we stop resisting our negative feelings, they may become powerless. Feelings gain their strength from resistance. When asked to join a war protest, Mother Teresa said the following: "I was once asked why I don't participate in anti-war demonstrations. I said that I will never do that, but as soon as you have a pro-peace rally, I'll be there."[8]

Gabriela from Costa Rica told me the following when I asked her about her decision to pursue happiness. "During a bad experience, there is a moment where I feel it is enough. It depends on the specific situation. For example, my daddy died suddenly at 60, just two days after his birthday. It was because a drunk guy crashed his car into him. I cried for months. I never talked about it until I accepted the pain as part of me and stopped suffering. On the other hand, I took care of my mum for years. She was like my baby, the role of mother-daughter reversed. I did everything I could for her but she died two years ago at 84! Instantly, I felt satisfied and understood that my mission, my duty with her, was complete. I continued my life without her easily and peacefully. If I hadn't confronted my pain when my dad died and refused, repressed, and denied what happened, I would have suffered longer and would not have been able to help my mother."

Darine from Egypt also divulged her tale of discovery. "I'd say my biggest obstacle was that I really believed I shouldn't be happy," she told me. "I told myself I felt better when I was sad and I think I still believe it on some level. It shouldn't be our aim to be 'happy', the mainstream happy that corresponds to smiling and being joyful or bubbly all the time. So, I guess what kind of solved that dilemma for me was actually redefining happiness, or just considering that happiness is not a one-size-fits-all thing. I was able to capture a personal definition that works for me, even if it makes no sense to others." Darine seemed to understand that happiness is different for everyone and was able to adapt the emotion to fit into her unique lifestyle.

Monica from Lima said the following about her experience. "I decided to be happy always. Sometimes it happens that I see myself focusing on feeling happy that I get tangled up with the idea of wanting to keep myself that way and it makes me unhappy. When I allow myself to be sad or angry or nervous or whatever appears, I appreciate my happiness and I also recognize the moment I am living."

These interviews prove that everyone is different and should pave their own path to happiness. You are just the same. Do what works for you because not every idea will relate or help everyone. Find your happiness your way.

Here are a couple of exercises we can practice whenever we feel a negative feeling.

1. When we have a feeling that we don't want to experience, we should not think about it. Instead, we should think of a happy memory or try to concentrate our thoughts on a positive feeling. We should start to listen to our inner thoughts; these thoughts are so powerful and infinite that they will manage to put us in a good mood. Focusing on positive thoughts will bring us positive feelings.

2. There is a very effective exercise which we can perform whenever we are having a negative feeling. We should determine which bad trait is trying to leave us so we can be better people. Experiencing a negative feeling is like having a physical infection; our bodies are trying to reject something harmful. For example, when we feel envious towards someone, we should think about why we feel that way or what our heart is trying to tell us. It could be because we compared ourselves to

another, meaning that our body is trying to tell us to stop comparing ourselves to other people. We have to feel grateful for the things we already have or we have to be wiser because maybe there is something we can't see. Maybe we are as good as that person but in another field. As time goes by, we will notice that it is a privilege to feel bad because feeling bad makes us notice the bad personality traits that are trying to leave us with a clean soul. Every time we feel bad, we become better people.

7. Stress Isn't Going to Solve Anything

THERE IS NO SITUATION that requires stress; I have tried to find an instance where stress is required but I did not find one. Don't get me wrong, some situations may require alertness but sometimes we just turn on the autopilot mood of being stressed, as if we feel we should be stressed at that moment of the day. We become stressed or upset for being stuck in a traffic jam or for being in a hurry. If we knew stress was not going to help us and that there was no need to be stressed, we could get rid of stress and calm ourselves down. We make better judgments and decisions when we are relaxed and in control of our emotions. Even in the most serious situations, if we are calm from the inside our performance will be better on the outside. The problem is that sometimes we confuse stress and productivity. We assume that the more stressed we are the more productive we will be, but this is not real. The more stressed we are the less productive we will be and the more relaxed we are the more productive we will be.

8. You Are Where You Are Supposed to Be:

THERE IS A FAMOUS TRAVELER and bestselling author named Robin Esrock who traveled to more than thirty-six countries. He did a TED Talk called "Learn to Travel—Travel to Learn"[9] where he recited the challenges he faced while he was traveling. One of the challenges he faced during his journey was his doubt. He always doubted the place he was in and whether it was the right place or not. He always felt that there was something missing until someone asked to borrow his bus ticket because he was having an emergency.

The bus got into an accident and the person died. That was when Robin realized he was where he was supposed to be. In our modern world, there are so many opportunities, professions, and experiences to the extent that they confuse us. We can see in one day the same number of job vacancies or business opportunities that a person fifty years ago saw in his lifetime. This abundance of opportunities is good but it creates a new kind of fear called "the fear of missing out". It is the fear of not taking an opportunity that may suit you in the future combined with the fear of not having the same opportunity again. To calm yourself down, you have to know that you are where you are supposed to be even if you are not where you wish to be. You can change where you are but you shouldn't be mad about it. Just accept it, trust it, and be determined to change it if you want.

9. You Are Not the Only Person Going Through This:

IT IS COMMON FOR PEOPLE who are unhappy due to loneliness, depression, or any other negative emotion to feel isolated. They feel like they are the only person on the planet that is experiencing that negative emotion, although the feeling of isolation makes the situation even worse. On the contrary, most people are experiencing moments of sadness, shame, loneliness, and unworthiness no matter how successful, happy, or wealthy they may appear. What differentiates between one person's happiness and another's is the ability to deal with these sad moments and how long they surrender to them. Knowing that it is normal to experience these negative emotions is the first step to accepting them; only then will they disappear.

10. Do Not Think About the Problem, Think About the Solution

THINKING ABOUT HOW and why the problem happened will never solve it; it will make you feel worse about it. In other words, we shouldn't keep blaming ourselves or others for having any problem. We should stop the "what ifs". We should think about the root of the problem so we can solve it. Thinking about the solution will make you feel better and in control. Do not underestimate any solution you have because, as long as you are trying, you will find the right one.

Anthony Robbins is an entrepreneur, bestselling author, philanthropist, and America's #1 life and business strategist. I once heard him talking about a training he had on how to drive a car like the drivers of Formula 1. While he was training to drive, the car went out of control and straight toward the wall; the trainer moved Anthony's head away from the wall and made him look at the other side. Consequently, Robbins turned the steering wheel and avoided the accident. The trainer told him that he can only go to the place he's looking to so if he had kept looking at the wall, he would have hit it. That's why the trainer made him look at the other side. If we start focusing on solutions rather than focusing on the problems, we will go towards the solutions and away from the problems.

11. Look for the Opportunity, Not the Obligation

THINKING ABOUT THE obligation in every situation will leave you powerless and sad, but thinking about the opportunity will boost your mood and unleash your creativity to make the most out of every situation. For example, if you don't like your job and want to quit but are not financially able to do so, you have the ability to make time and study something that brings you happiness and that can eventually bring you monetary gain. In every situation, there is an opportunity and there is an obligation. If we focused on the obligation, saying that we have no choice and that we are forced to do it, we will end up depressed and powerless. If we looked for the opportunity in the situation, we would feel proactive, creative, and fulfilled.

12. Don't Attach Your Happiness to a Goal

HAPPINESS GETS KICKED into the future; it is not always there but will eventually surface. Happiness is a state of mind, not a goal. Don't fall into the trap of "when I achieve that goal I will be happy". You might be happier when you achieve that goal but don't make your happiness depend on it. When you achieve that goal, another will take its place and it will turn into a never-ending journey to achieve happiness.

In our modern world, most of the advertising and marketing campaigns are designed to not only fulfill a need but to create one that we didn't have in the first place. If you wait for an achievement to be happy, you won't be because there will always be another goal. At times there may even be a goal that we pursue but it turns out to be an illusion, an imaginary goal that was created by social media.

We keep pushing our happiness to the future because our imagination is stronger than reality. The picture we draw in our minds is more beautiful than it appears so we keep feeling stressed or bad, waiting for the miracle to happen, wasting our lives and neglecting special moments that are waiting to be lived.

The fact that you need to do something to be happy reinforces the assumption that you are unhappy. What if we assume that our default state is happiness? What if we make happiness a place where we move from, not a place we move to? Happiness should be something we feel, not something we are trying to reach. There are a lot of thoughts that deter us from reaching our goals, like "What if we die before reaching our goal?" or "What if a better opportunity comes along?"

If we choose to be happy, we are more likely to achieve our goals because when we are happy our mental and physical performance increases significantly. Happiness always brings happiness, so if you are feeling happy now then it is more likely that you'll be happy in the near future.

There are two types of happiness: natural happiness and synthetic happiness. Natural happiness is what we feel when we get what we want. Synthetic happiness is what we do when we don't get what we want. It is all about our attitude towards setbacks and difficulties when we don't achieve what we aim for. The media has made us believe that we can't be happy unless we get what we want so they can create never-ending needs. Although those needs aren't real, we don't actually feel happy unless we satisfy them. If we realized that happiness wasn't exclusively limited to getting what we want and that we could easily be happy regardless of our needs' satisfaction, we may find our way to happiness without getting what we think we need to be happy. Do not get me wrong, I am not talking about basic needs like food, water, shelter, or clothes. I am talking about the possessions or experiences we can live without but feel we need because we are conditioned to rely on them.

13. You Deserve Happiness

SOMETIMES WE FEEL LIKE we don't deserve good things in life or that we have to have permission before experiencing something pleasant. This can be caused by different reasons and it differs from one person to another. During the pursuit of this permission, we travel, gain certificates, and accumulate money, thinking that when we do this or when we possess something so important we will deserve to be happy or we will have the permission to be happy. But how do we overcome this feeling?

Whenever we get this feeling, the feeling of unworthiness of happiness, we should ask ourselves some questions. Who deserves to be happy? What is the criterion of a happy person? What is the point which a man must reach in order to be happy? What is this specific thing that I must do in order to deserve happiness? Which person or entity gives permission for someone to be happy and another to be unhappy? If it is not you, who is making an effort by reading a book about happiness and searching for ways to live happier? Who deserves it?

Sometimes we don't notice the effort we make at a certain point in our lives or maybe we underestimate it. If you focus on the effort you made up to that thing and it doesn't satisfy you, you will see that you have done a pretty good job. Maybe it's not enough, but it is sufficient for you to deserve happiness and to give yourself the permission to be happy. If there is no person or entity which gives us the permission to be happy, why don't we give it to ourselves?

Part Two:
Happy Actions

I n this part, I will share specific actions you can take to bring happiness into your life. A few of my interviewees reflected on their journey and their stories can be followed below.

Anna from Munich noted the following when asked about why she chose to take control of her life and become happy. "I have been working on improving my happiness scale for some time. Last year I quit my job and I did some work on self-confidence and self-coaching. I participated in the Science of Happiness. I feel that almost everyone can become at least a bit happier—if they change their focus or really look into themselves to find out what really makes them happy."

Mel from Canada also noted her fluctuations in mood. "I have experienced spurts of depression throughout my life and lost a sense of who I was for a long time. It wasn't until my father passed away that I really started questioning the meaning of my life. I was tired of always feeling alone and unloved like I wasn't good enough for anyone or anything. So, I started listening to Louise Hay affirmations on my drive to work. It just exploded from there. I changed my entire Facebook feed to only reflect positive quotes, inspiring messages, and mindset challenges. I dove into my yoga practice on a new, spiritual level. I started caring about my body and started journaling and exploring my emotions and who I am as a person."

Yasmine from Egypt had something profound to say about happiness. "Being happy requires self-discipline. It takes a lot of work. I increased my happiness by working on my personal growth." We can all learn from Yasmine; finding happiness takes effort and determination.

14. It's Not as Scary as It Looks

I FEEL IMPRESSED WHEN I remember how many times I was afraid to do something that appeared so difficult and scary at the time but turned out to be very easy when done. Nothing is as painful or scary as it appears to be. I wonder how many trips, meetings, friendships, seminars, and adventures I would have missed if I didn't find the courage to take action. I am not talking about committing crazy acts without keeping the consequences in mind; I am talking about the unreasonable fear we face when we are about to do something new, knowing that it may require us to get out of our comfort zones. We then think of each possible scenario. We know we are ready to do something by listening to our inner thoughts. We sometimes get scared because our mind only measures the amount of any possible loss and neglects the amount we could gain, but if we thought about what we would gain from doing the things we want to do, the benefits would be infinite.

After reading this, you should try to do one thing that you are afraid of doing and then count the things you gained from it. You will realize there are lots of gains and that the positives were unpredictable. You'll notice that the things you were afraid of happening never happened.

15. You Are Not a Machine

SOMETIMES WE BLAME ourselves for being stressed, tired, or sad because we keep telling ourselves that we should be much stronger, neglecting the fact that we are humans that have emotions and feelings and that it is normal to be affected to life's events. We have a certain amount of energy that needs to be recharged before we can get back on track. Stop being so hard on yourself and start to be more self-aware. How much energy can you spend throughout the day? How many hours can you work? How many hours of sleep do you need to be active throughout the day? What things should you avoid because they absorb your energy? When you become aware of these things, you'll start to make goals that match your capabilities and will start to avoid the persons and situations that absorb your energy.

16. Do One Thing at a Time

AS THE FORMS OF MEDIA increase, every new form steals time and attention from the previous one. Radio stole time from newspapers, television stole time from the radio, the internet stole time from all the above. They created a world of distraction. Some people call it the attention economy, where everybody wants your attention and you can become easily distracted. We can be reached twenty-four hours a day, seven days a week through numerous channels of communication, which I consider a privilege. But at the same time, we have to control when we get exposed to these channels. We must not waste all our time checking social media platforms; we may get notifications that are not important or can be delayed for a while, like a comment from a friend on your profile picture or a friend sending a joke through WhatsApp. Before we even notice, hours pass by in a flash, with nothing to show for our time.

Due to the time wasted on social media, we try to do more things quickly and in less time, which is a function our minds are not designed for. It is easy to figure out that multitasking is a myth; it affects our productivity, creativity, the quality of our work, and our mental health. Multitasking distributes your attention by focusing on more than one thing and not finishing any. It leaves you tired and stressed. Our brains need more time and full engagement to fully function and process information. Multitasking requires our minds to focus on more than one task at the same time, processing the information of each task solely then moving on to the next task. In order to avoid a headache, try to rest your mind and do one thing at a time. Adjust your work environment so you have no distractions because when we are exposed to distractions we have to make a decision. Whether this decision is to avoid them or to focus on them, it requires mental energy to choose. By working in a peaceful place with no distractions, we minimize the number of decisions we make during our working hours.

When I have something important to work on, I go to a place where no one can interrupt me, like a coworking space. I switch off my mobile and disable the internet if I am working on something offline. If not, I try to close all the websites that may interrupt me. Don't be afraid to miss anything; you will always have time to check those notifications when you are on the subway or waiting for a friend in a coffee shop. It's a never-ending cycle; there will always be notifications to check on your phone. If necessary, dedicate time to browse your social media accounts, maybe half an hour before going to sleep. Focusing on one thing at a time will allow you to make progress. It will become a habit and you will be internally motivated by the progress you make when you get focused. The distraction of the new age of communication may waste your time and energy without accomplishing what you want, which leads to the depression that affects your happiness. Focusing on one thing at a time will bring you more progress and satisfaction.

17. Appreciate What You Have

THE MOST COMMON MISTAKE we make is not appreciating what we have; we always look forward to what we don't have. If you want to be happy, you have to appreciate what you have because we all have uncountable blessings which we tend to neglect. If we stopped to imagine our lives without these blessings, we may appreciate them. Neuroscience has proven that even if you have nothing you can still show gratitude by being grateful. Showing gratitude helps you become happier. As silly as it may sound, whenever I feel unhappy I ask myself, "What if I was blind and I just got my sight back? How would I feel?" Chasing the things we don't have should not make us lose sight or stop enjoying the things that we do have.

When I asked one of my interviewees, David, about what he eliminated from his life in order to be happy, he responded with the following about his outlook on life: "Last year I attended an ayahuasca ceremony in my city which was a peak experience that confronted me with my ego and my bad emotions and revealed to me all the positive emotions and beautiful things that already exist in my life. I learned that I took many things for granted and I appreciate them now."

In our modern world, we have a lot of things to be grateful for, like the internet. The internet made the human experience better than ever before with the business opportunities it gives, the knowledge it offers for free, the relations it has enhanced, and the opportunities it gave people to share and support each other no matter how far apart they are.

Many of my interviewees divulged their experiences with a gratitude list. Darine from Egypt discussed her experience, which may put your mind at ease. "I tried to be more aware of what makes me happy," she told me. "Having a gratitude diary helped a lot (even though I wasn't writing religiously), and having that awareness helped me appreciate the good things when they happened—not afterward. It also helped to recreate joyful and fulfilling experiences when needed."

Mel from Canada also had some wisdom to share. "I started a gratitude journal that helped pull me out of a dark period. For six months, I wrote ten things I appreciated in my life before bed. This was the major catalyst that started to shift my thinking."

Krista from St. Louis was ecstatic about the idea of a journal. "I've also been practicing some form of gratitude every day from the book *Magic* and I'm seeing the law of attraction come quickly into effect!"

Keeping a gratitude list is a simple exercise that may help you feel grateful for what you have in life. You may write a daily list before going to sleep or after waking up that contains three things for which you are grateful. When tested on a number of students, they found their happiness and satisfaction levels increased significantly.

18. Transform Your Anger into Positive Energy

IT IS EASIER SAID THAN done, but we all have a certain level of anger and it decreases if your quality of life increases. In order to prevent this anger from destroying us, we have to find something that can affect our lives positively and put our anger into it. Whenever I feel stressed or depressed, I go jogging for one hour because anger is a strong feeling that contains a huge amount of energy. It can either make or destroy our lives, so if we have the ability to employ our anger and transform it into positive energy, we can use that energy to achieve more.

First, you have to know exactly what is making you angry. You have to look deep inside and find the real cause of your anger; it's not caused by a ridiculous situation, as it may appear. A situation may have provoked it but it's not the real cause behind it. Second, you should find a way to control your anger by getting over the things that make you angry. Third, consider all the actions you may take in order to help you get over the situation that caused your anger. If you don't know what those actions are, you have to do a little research to find out.

For example, I was unhappy with my job and my unhappiness was the main cause of my anger. Anger comes to the surface only when something triggers it. I started to look for the things that I enjoyed doing and made a long-term plan to start profiting from the things that I loved. Your cause of anger may be something else; it may be that you are always tired, so you should make a plan including more rest time. It may be that you are stuck in a toxic relationship and you have to choose either to confront your partner with what bothers you or to end the relationship. The actions that must be taken to get rid of your anger will be determined by the cause of the anger.

Finally, whenever you feel angry, do some of the long-term actions you have determined in the third step; you will notice that your anger will decrease and someday the situation that has always made you angry will finally disappear.

I have decided that writing is the action I should take to change the situation that makes me angry. It took me a while to rewire my brain to put my anger into writing, but with persistence I made it. Jack Canfield, an award-winning speaker and internationally recognized leader in personal development and peak performance strategies, said the following:

> In order to complain about something or someone, you have to believe that something better exists. You have to have a reference point of something you prefer that you are not willing to take responsibility for creating. Think about this... people only complain about things they can do something about. We don't complain about the things we have no power over. Have you ever heard anyone complain about gravity? Of course not. [10]

So next time you complain, remember you can change your anger into something positive.

19. Tame Your Brain

OUR BRAINS ARE ALWAYS working; they always want to achieve something, so if we are not using them properly they will create challenges for us. The problem is that our brains crave a problem to solve. I tame my brain by doing two things: meditation and consistent action. Meditation is a state of mind; it is a huge and powerful prescription. Some of the benefits of meditation are difficult to describe to someone who has never tried it; however, there are some positive attributes that are easy to notice, even as an observer. One of the benefits of meditation is rejuvenation; it reboots your mind. Practicing meditation will help you tackle the excessive thinking problem. But meditation is not the only way to tame your brain.

A consistent action is an action that you consistently do, which tends to be meaningful, pleasurable, and positive. Your mind will be satisfied that it is achieving a positive result regularly. But the consistent action doesn't have to be a big thing; it could be something as simple as writing a note on your mobile, initiating a conversation with a stranger, taking a good photo, or calling someone who you have not talked to for a while. Just engage your mind in something positive consistently.

20. Evaluate Your Life

IF YOU ARE NOT HAPPY most of the time, then I advise you to evaluate your health, relationships, career, finances, and anything else in your life you focus on daily. Find ways to improve those parts of your life by taking very small steps in each one. Looking for ways to improve these areas will bring you satisfaction, and here is a very useful link to help you. It contains a group of questionnaires created by the University of Pennsylvania. It will help you measure the level of your happiness and evaluate your life.

https://www.authentichappiness.sas.upenn.edu/testcenter

21. Make Your Own List

THERE ARE NUMEROUS reasons why happiness varies from person to person. Some events can make one person sad and another one happy; that's why you have to be more conscious of what makes you happy and what brings joy to your life. Whenever you feel happy, try to record it on your mobile or write it on a piece of paper. Then, after a while, you will have a list of the things that bring happiness into your life. Whenever you feel sad, you can check this list and choose the easiest thing to help you get over your bad mood. Along the journey, you may adjust this list; you can remove or add things, making it more complex or simpler.

22. Have a To-Be List

MOST OF US HAVE A TO-do list, whether written or in mind, that contains big goals or insignificant ones, daily activities, or something material that we want to achieve. It is not something bad, but what if in addition to this to-do list you also had a to-be list that included the characteristics and qualities that you wanted to acquire?

First, why should we have a to-be list? We should have one because it's our personalities that matter; they determine the quality of our lives. For example, if you are a sociable person and you want to communicate with people to enhance your business, it would be much easier if you were an extrovert. Here is another example: An optimistic person would overcome life's challenges more effectively than a pessimistic person. In conclusion, two different persons may have the same experience but their personalities will allow one of them to get more out of the experience than the other. Most of the people who have won the lottery ended up going broke within one to three years after winning because they didn't have the required personality traits that would have qualified them to keep, or even increase, their fortune. This example shows that we could have the money, the relationship, or any other thing that we desire; however, even if we were lucky enough to obtain it, we would end up losing it because of who we are and the personality traits we have.

How do we make a to-be list? Try to define the qualities you want to acquire. This can be done through two methods. First, identify the characteristics which you don't like about your personality and try to improve them. For example, if you don't like being hesitant, you should change that by trying to be more certain. The second method is to think logically about what your close ones tell you. What are their major complaints about you? Then think about whether these complaints are real or not by comparing them to your actions and intentions. If they match and you decide you really want to change them, put those characteristics into the to-be list.

Sometimes the people closest to us feel the willingness to change something about us, something we already like or is unique. Don't decide to change any of your qualities because someone said that it has to be changed.

After making the to-be list, imagine how a person acquiring the quality in which you desire would behave and then train yourself to behave the same. For example, most people were telling me that I was stingy and I noticed that it might be true. Consequently, I decided to change this quality. I monitored the people who I felt were generous and I copied their actions. I've since found that it is easy to be generous; whenever I am called stingy, I don't care because now I know it is not true.

What is the quality that you want to acquire? Do you want to be a better father or mother, a better husband or son, a better student? Do you want to be more conscious, sociable, generous, resilient, or brave? Who do you know that has these qualities? Monitor them and imitate them.

23. Determine What You Want

WHAT YOU WANT DOESN'T have to be a huge goal or a vision board; it can be a simple desire. When you wake up in the morning, try to think of two or three things you want to accomplish that day. You may write them on a piece of paper and put it in your pocket or write it as a reminder on your phone to remind you as you go. Applying this action to your daily life will make you feel more confident and content.

I believe that if people worked more on what they really wanted, they wouldn't have to work so hard. We waste a lot of time and energy on things we don't want. We have been turning on autopilot and doing things without asking ourselves whether they are really beneficial to us or if they make us happy. If we decided to act more consciously and purposefully, we would realize that there are so many things which we can give up. If we started this on a small level, like focusing on the small tasks that we want to do, it will gradually affect our lives, giving us the life we really want.

24. Legacy Is Better Than Currency

THINKING ABOUT YOUR grandchildren. What would they think of you? Would they be proud of you? Would they even remember you? Take Gandhi and Mother Teresa as examples. They did not leave a lot of money to their inheritors but they left a legacy that was more precious than money. They left their legacies by following their hearts and being true to themselves. Prophet Muhammad PBUH was once told to stop spreading his message; in return, they promised to crown him as king and marry him to the most beautiful girl in town. But he rejected.

Believe in your message; stay true to yourself. As time goes by, you will not regret the money you did not make but you will regret the risks you did not take. Ask yourself what legacy you want to leave when you are dead. What are the things you want people to remember you by? What can you do to leave the most positive impact on the world?

25. Have a Meaningful and Pleasurable Goal

BENJAMIN E. MAYS, A great civil rights leader, and Baptist, once said that "the tragedy of life doesn't lie in not reaching goals; the tragedy of life lies in not having any goals to reach. It is not a calamity to die with unachieved dreams, but it's a calamity not to dream."[11] Only having a meaningful goal that wakes you up every day will make you feel confident and worthwhile. On the other hand, don't forget that it's you who set the goal in the first place, so the purpose is not the goal itself. The purpose is to have a goal.

If setting a goal is making you less happy, try adjusting the techniques and the methods to make the process more enjoyable and pleasurable. If nothing works, try to evaluate your goal. Is it still meaningful? If it is meaningful, it is going to be enjoyable and pleasurable. You should always enjoy your work. Find something that brings happiness to you and others. This goal has to be meaningful to you, not to your family or friends because reaching a goal that is not meaningful to you will not make you feel happy or satisfied. On the contrary, it will make you feel lonely, as everybody will see you as a successful person but you won't feel like one.

I experienced this when I worked as a judge. As you know, it is a very prestigious and respectful profession, so whenever I tell people I am not satisfied with my job, that I have more to offer, that my job is not challenging enough for me, and it is not motivating me to improve myself, they tell me that I should be grateful for having such a good job and they make me feel guilty for expressing my feelings. They question me when I say that working as a judge does not mean a lot to me. This is an example of how you can have a goal that means everything to others but does not mean a lot to you. When you start to pursue a meaningful and pleasurable goal, you begin to respect and love yourself more. You begin to live by new standards. You begin to get rid of your bad habits and become more disciplined; this is how your self-worth increases.

Your life becomes more valuable to you. Consequently, you begin to take care of your body and pay attention to how you spend your time because you have something valuable to deliver to the world. As soon as you begin to take serious steps towards something that is really meaningful to you, you will find followers who believe in you. You will feel responsible for them and they will see you as a role model. You don't want to disappoint them or yourself.

How do you know what is meaningful to you? There is an exercise that can help you envision what is meaningful to you. Take twelve photos of what you think is meaningful to you in a one-month period. After taking those pictures, discuss them with a close friend or family member, think about the reason behind their importance to you, and set some goals around the things that you found.

Khaled, an interviewee from Cairo, talked to me about his obstacles and how he overcame them. "I was in the hospital during finals in college and I got bad grades on the midterms, so I said to my father, 'Look, I will prove myself and get better grades,'" he told me. "So, when I went to the hospital, he said he could understand if I got bad grades. The grades came out and I got four A's and one A-minus. I was so happy and grateful that I went to the hospital because it made me believe that everything happens for a reason and anything is possible once you put your mind to it."

When enjoyment and importance are combined in an action, the action is going to bring us happiness. Unfortunately, it's difficult to find those kinds of actions that are enjoyable and important at the same time. Some actions are enjoyable but not important, like lying on the beach. Others are important but not enjoyable, like studying hard for an academic degree. However, when the challenge of not finding enjoyment in an important action faces you, you can start thinking about life in macros. Look at the future benefits of that action. When the opposite happens, when it's not important but it's enjoyable, think of your present status and enjoy every second of it, as not every moment should be meaningful or of importance. Sometimes we have to do something that only brings joy to our lives.

26. Do Something for Yourself

I DON'T HAVE A PROBLEM with working for someone else, or with being a civil servant, but doing something for yourself is the best thing you can do. It does not have to be profitable, but it has to be something you enjoy doing. It could be a small thing, like reading, drawing, or jogging, but you should dedicate some time to it in order to make yourself happy. While doing this thing, you should ask yourself whether it still makes you happy or not. If not, try something else. The thing you do for yourself could be seen as weird by many people. It does not matter what everybody thinks, as long as it makes you happy.

27. Happiness is a Muscle

IF YOU ARE NOT HAPPY with your life and you are trying to be happy, let me be the one who tells you the bad news you are not going to find happiness in one night; it is a process made up of small shifts that build the proper mindsets, habits, and feelings. You must train yourself to focus on taking positive actions; you must also try to train yourself to manage your feelings and to know how to deal with them. Our brains are very good with habits; they get better and better at the things we repetitively do. If we trained our brains to be happier, they would get better at being happy. If we trained them to be sad and miserable, they would also be better at being so.

Additionally, when you start to train yourself to focus on the positive and to deal with your feelings and suddenly stop, such stopping will gradually make you lose the strength of the happiness muscle that you have worked so hard to build. Accordingly, you have to keep that positive discipline in your life. For example, I have started a 30-day challenge where I choose three or four positive actions to do daily and evaluate those actions and how they have changed my life after the 30 days so I can create the next challenge more effectively. Some days I don't do any of those actions; I just continue the challenge, forgiving myself and sometimes revisiting the actions of the previous day.

Like me, Monica from Lima created a routine in her daily life to remind herself to stay positive. "One of my happiest memories occurred when I was in college twenty-two years ago and I found an advertisement that said 'Be happy. Eat an M&M'. I took it and put it on the wall of my room. It was a happy yellow face, like an emoticon. From that moment, I began to add the phrase 'Be happy' to my signatures and many years later it became my purpose to inspire other people to be happy. If someone asks me what I do, I respond with 'Be happy.'"

Monica strengthened her happiness muscle by putting a picture in her room and reminding herself every day to be happy. How would you strengthen your happiness muscle? You can put a background on your mobile or create an alarm to remind yourself to evaluate your mood. If you have a positive routine, even if you don't do it for one or two days for some reason, keep doing it.

28. Be Balanced

DURING A COACHING SESSION given by a life coach named Islam Ayoub, I learned that the life of a human being is like a triangle. At the first summit is the mind; anything related to your job, readings, and other intellectual activities can be found there. The second summit is the body; it includes any physical activity or healthy food habits. The last one is the heart and it includes family and friends, gatherings, and any other emotional activity that may occur. In the center of the triangle is the soul that feeds the three summits. In life, we should do more activities that feed the three aspects of our lives in order to feel fulfilled and happy. It does not have to be a huge activity.

We can take me as an example. Whenever I'm having a bad day or feeling depressed, I read something that nurtures my mind, watch a TED Talk, and then work out, sit with my family, or go out to meet some friends. So, consequently, the way I feel changes dramatically. It is not noble or smart to live only serving one summit and neglecting the other two; on the contrary, this is when we feel sad or unbalanced. Having a balance between all three summits creates happiness and fulfillment. Now, when you feel sad or depressed, search for the side that you are neglecting and nurture it; your mood will positively change.

29. Be Congruent

CONGRUENCE SIMPLY MEANS that what we think, feel, say, and do are consistent. Gandhi said you shouldn't do things that contradict your thoughts, values, or feelings because it will lower your self-esteem. I know this is easier said than done, but try to be aware in every situation. Try your best to be as congruent as possible. A happy person should be congruent but a congruent person may not be happy. You may not be happy after achieving congruence because your true self is not familiar with happiness. Accordingly, you should develop other habits, mindsets, and philosophies that lead to happiness. If you want to achieve something in order to be happy, you must know that you are changing to please yourself, not others. If you only want to change to please other people, you will never be happy and you will never be satisfied.

30. Have Faith

THERE ARE NUMEROUS things in life that we cannot control, no matter how hard we try, so if we do not believe that there is something greater than ourselves, something that is controlling those things, life will never make sense to us.

Amany from Egypt told me about the time she found happiness: "I don't have a specific story, but in general we all have our ups and downs. I went through bad times like every human being and with every down, I got closer to God. I pray to God and I talk with him about my problems. When you get closer to God and realize he is your number-one best friend, you feel safe and peaceful and of course, this feeling brings happiness."

By believing that there is something controlling the universe, like an omnipotent God who has plans for all of us, we begin to calm down and believe there is a reason behind everything, even if we don't realize it right away.

31. Watch Your Body Gestures

I ONCE SAW AN INTERESTING TED Talk called "Your Body Language Shapes Who You Are" by Amy Cuddy.[12] She talked about how you can control how you feel by changing your physiology. She was talking about the power of poses. The power of poses refers to the body poses that trigger the confidence hormones in our bodies. You cannot be happy without projecting the image of happiness. For example, when you feel depressed or sad, watch your body gestures; it is likely that you will notice your shoulders and neck are slumped downwards and your body is contorting.

Why don't we make the happiness poses? The happiness poses are whatever poses that make your body expand with a smile on your face, like lying on the floor opening your arms and legs wide. This works both ways; when you change your body gestures, your mood improves and when your mood improves, your body gestures change.

32. Anchor Your Happiness

IN NLP (NEURO-LINGUISTIC programming), there is something called anchoring, which is a built-in quality of human beings. Anchoring is an unconscious response we have to a physical motion, sound, picture, smell, taste, or any other external stimulus. You might have a song that reminds you of someone, someplace, or an event, a smell that makes you feel hungry, or a movie that reminds you of a certain time or setup. Anchors might be positive or negative. You might have a song that reminds you of negative memories or makes you sad and another one that reminds you of good memories or makes you happy. What if we use this built-in quality to our favor, instead of letting it remind us of sad events and memories? We can use it to trigger any positive emotion we want. What if we could evoke any feeling we wanted and at any desirable time?

The next steps will teach you how to do just that.

1. Reimagine a situation where you felt the feeling you want to remember now. Reimagine everything: the sound, the smell, the way you were standing. Recall every single detail as if you were experiencing it for the first time until you capture the intense feeling of the situation.

2. Make any physical motion you'd like while feeling this intense, positive feeling. It should not be a big or weird motion; it should be a motion you can make in public when you want to trigger that feeling again. It could be a very simple move, like tightening your fist, tapping on your leg, or touching one hand with the other.

3. Repeat this process three to four times and then test it by making that move without evoking the situation. You should get the same feeling that you had during that situation. If you are not getting the same feeling, repeat the process until you notice that the feeling is anchored to that move.

33. Be Steadfast

I HAVE ALWAYS WONDERED how some people could be so steadfast; some people are patient and they don't bother wondering about the future. I always wanted to acquire that skill until I realized it was not something you acquired but something that was within you. You only have to stop and allow it to flow through you. You can just say "stop", take a deep breath, say "allow", and then feel the steadiness flow within you. You can repeat this exercise whenever you are in a rush or whenever you want to calm yourself down. This exercise can help you when you want something badly but you don't want anybody to notice your eagerness.

When we are more steadfast, we become stronger. If you try to throw a stick to a dog, he will instantly and briskly run to catch it. If you try to throw a stick to a lion, he will stand still and look to see where it came from to determine whether it is worth the chase or not.

This could also help in sales and during business meetings when you don't want to let the other person know his offer is too good to be true. The problem is we go for whatever comes in front of us without thinking about whether it is beneficial and useful to us. If we stand still for a moment before acting or reacting to the things we see, hear, or feel, we will make better decisions acting as lions, not dogs.

34. Your Happy Version

IMAGINE YOU ACHIEVED the level of happiness you desire. What would you feel? How would you dress? How would you talk, walk, and eat? What would your lifestyle be like? Imagine every single detail, no matter how insignificant you think it is, and write it down. Close your eyes and visualize yourself living that day. Try to do the things that bring you closer to the happy version of yourself. I know it is not that easy, because if it were that happy version of you would already exist. Developing happy habits will bring you closer to the happy version which you visualized.

35. Live Like You are Driving

IMAGINE WE ARE LIVING the same way that we drive our cars, motorcycles, and bicycles. At first we have to be humble and learn from someone, then we have to get out of our comfort zones and put ourselves behind the steering wheel and drive because there is no other way to learn how to do it. We don't have to know everything about the vehicle or the road, we just have to keep moving, even if we're going in the wrong direction. We ask for help if we stumble, we fix ourselves as quickly as possible, and then we keep going. In driving, the one who knows his destination and focuses on it is the one who is going to reach it the fastest.

If someone insulted us while we were driving and we ignored him, we would reach our destination faster and with no harm. If we focused on his insults, we would be obstructed and may lose our focus. In driving, if we find a road that is blocked, we don't change our destination; we just change our path to it. If our vehicle is not fully prepared for the journey, it may stop along the way, so we have to make sure we are fully prepared and have the capabilities and the faith that will take us to the place we desire.

If something goes wrong with our vehicle along the journey, we don't think about why it happened and we don't complain about it or analyze it, we just focus on the solution. If there is a dual way and the cars are coming in the opposite direction, we just have to trust that the other drivers will not jump in front of us and cause an accident.

We also have to apply this to our relationships; we have to trust our partners until they do something wrong. We usually think negatively about our relationships, especially in the beginning. Sometimes we make mistakes while driving; these mistakes will not only harm us, they will also harm other people. We need to make our choices carefully. We should never get in a vehicle with a driver who is irresponsible. If we are going to put our lives in another person's hands, we have to make sure they are capable of keeping us safe.

Accidents may happen, and sometimes we don't have anything to do with them, but we have to accept them anyway. The thing that differs from a winner and a loser is who gets to stand up and keep going. If we applied these lessons to our lives, we would live happily and positively. Next time you use transportation, try to remember these lessons and let it inspire you. You will never see transportation the same again.

36. Use Every Opportunity to Overcome Your Sadness

SOMETIMES WE ARE SAD, and there are millions of reasons behind our sadness, but I don't care why you are sad; there is nothing wrong with being sad. The problem occurs when we have a chance to get over our sadness and we refuse it. If someone called you while you felt sad, hopeless, or despaired and asked you to join him/her in an outing, project, or even a ride, don't refuse. No matter how bad you feel, take advantage of these moments; they will help you overcome your sadness and you will feel positively different. You will even forget why you were sad.

37. Say "YES" More Often

SAYING "YES" WILL RESULT in new experiences, even if the experiences are bad. Saying "yes" will lead to a wiser "no" next time you are asked to join in the same experience. Saying "yes" and taking a risk, even if you feel like you will hate it, is way better than wondering what would have happened if you said "yes".

38. Consider Minimalism

WRITE A LIST OF THE ten most expensive things you own and find your happy list which we mentioned in Idea 23. Compare the lists and determine whether there are any similarities between them. Then cover all the furniture in your home and don't uncover anything unless you want to use it.

I got these ideas from a movement called "Minimalism" founded by Joshua Fields Millburn and Ryan Nicodemus from Ohio. They state that "minimalism is a tool to rid yourself of life's excess in favor of focusing on what's important so you can find happiness, fulfillment, and freedom."[13] When I applied minimalism, I didn't just start to get rid of the excess things I owned, I also got rid of my commitment towards those things. I'm not attached to any of them anymore. They no longer define or identify me.

Abd Allah from Cairo gave a very inspiring story about his conversion from consumerism to minimalism: "One day there was a problem with my internet connection and I was quite bored, as I was used to watching movies or an episode of my favorite show. To be honest, I usually watched two or three episodes a night but it always left me full of guilt. I wasted so much time and quite often did it to numb my brain and escape reality. That day, I played an episode that I watched before and I was really bored. I realized that I was living in a matrix. I was addicted. I was just trying to distract myself from my everyday struggles. I started to understand that I needed to wake up, to stay away from distractions, and to spend time according to my priorities. I started to see that everything around us is built to distract us. It is called the ENTERTAINMENT industry. Its main aim is to capture our attention. They plant specific ideas about success and happiness so that we consume more and they make more money. I started to realize that the first step to achieving inner peace is to stay away from distractions."

If we let our possessions identify us, we are going to lose ourselves whenever we lose one of them. This is the reason why we hear of people committing suicide after losing their money in the stock market or in a business; they were so attached to their possessions that they would rather die than lose them. Sometimes we make the same mistake but on a smaller level, until our possessions own us. So I encourage you to ask yourself this question: Do I own my belongings or do they own me?

39. Do Not Let Anything Define You, Other Than You

I DON'T KNOW WHO YOU are, but I know who you are not. You are not defined by your feelings because you have been through so many emotions and survived them all. We cannot define you by any of them.

You are not defined by your beliefs because your beliefs vary with time. As you age, your beliefs and your thoughts will keep changing. You may believe in something now that you once thought was a myth; that's why you cannot be defined by your beliefs.

You are not defined by your body; you were once a child with a very small body, a young man with a very strong build, or even an old man with a frail body. Maybe you have been very skinny or very fat. Maybe you have lost or gained some weight. You have lived through all these bodies, so obviously you are not your body.

You are not defined by your job, even if you have the same job for a very long time. You had a life before it and you will also have a life after it, so you are not your business, your job, or your position.

You are not defined by your money; money is a variable that changes over time. You may have a lot now and nothing later, so no one can define you by the amount of money you have.

You are not defined by your relationships, I give myself this advice whenever I'm having trouble facing a relationship problem. Whether losing or breaking up with someone, I had a life before and I'll always have one, so a relationship can never define who I am. You are bigger than those things; you can live through and experience all these feelings, beliefs, body shapes, jobs, and relationships without being defined by any of them.

We prevent ourselves from being happy by imprisoning ourselves in our own identities. In other words, the marks, positions, and titles we have sometimes prevent us from doing the things we love. You are the only one that can define who you are and that shall not stop you from being happy.

Every once in a while you have to do something new, something adventurous, to determine whether your position or your identity is holding you back from being free and happy. It does not have to be a big thing; it could be talking to a stranger, learning something new, or even getting a new haircut. Working as a judge made me feel like I was stuck with an identity. People always expected me to behave a certain way, to be satisfied with my position, and believed I did not have the right to have outside hobbies or interests. I was expected to be appreciative of my position, which I am, but I believe I can do something bigger. I attended a training session about project management and one of the attendees asked me what I was doing there after finding out I was a judge. I always thought that I could do more and I always wanted to do something else, so I began to attend seminars and courses that were related to the things I love. I began to attend coaching sessions that guided me and motivated me, I began to make new friends that believed in me and believed that I could do well with something else, and I began to go places where everyone was so welcoming and believed there was more in life. That helped me gain another identity that is more real and true to myself.

40. Capture the Moment

TAKE A PHOTO WHEN YOU are happy or are with a group of friends and/ or family, one that shows how you are really connected with them. Capturing these moments and returning to them will bring you the same feeling you had while taking it. It will put a smile on your face whenever you feel lonely or depressed.

Part Three:
Happy Body

I n this part, I will share some practical ideas on how to treat your body in order to achieve happiness.

41. Eat Happy Food

YOU MAY BE FAMILIAR with the videos on social media that feature molten chocolate cakes or photos of well-made pizzas; in the description for most of these videos, the word happiness can be found. People confuse what can make them happy now and what can make them happy forever. They confuse happiness with pleasure. When we eat the food we see in those pictures or videos, we are happy only while we are eating them. Once they have passed through our mouth, they start to make us uncomfortable because of the amount of sugar and fats they include. They also make us fat, which makes us feel uncomfortable about our bodies.

Our food and beverage choices are related to our happiness. If we are sick, it is much harder to be happy. I am not saying that you cannot be happy if you are sick, but it takes much more effort to be happy. As J.J. Virgin, the author of the bestselling book *The Virgin Diet* said, "food is messages." We cannot separate the brain from the body and there are always messages that go both ways; our brains send information to our bodies and our bodies send information to our brains. It is a never-ending process until the day we die. We can manage the quality of the messages our bodies are sending to our brains by controlling the quality of the food we eat.

Eric Edmeades, the founder of WildFit, determined that there are six hungers, or six core reasons, why people eat. One of them is "Emotional

Hunger". The problem with emotion-based eating decisions is that people often end up eating dysfunctional foods because they hope that those foods will help them feel better or, frankly, be happier.

A person might, for instance, feel a bit low and turn to chocolate to help them feel better and, for a fleeting moment, it might. But, sadly, non-functional foods (like those with excessive sugars) have the opposite effect in the long term. This, of course, can lead to a cycle of eating more and more of the wrong foods in an ever failing attempt to chase happiness.

The connection between proper hydration, breathing, and food cannot be understated. Eric Edmeades, the founder of WildFit, told me that, "In a survey of 400 people who spent three months changing their relationship with food, we found that the top three benefits they received were weight loss, an improved relationship with food, and a better sense of well being. When we asked people to explain their answer, the truth became clear: they were happier."

Eric suggested that there is a direct relationship between health and happiness. "When people are malnourished, it is safer for them to be pessimistic about life."

There are so many foods and drinks that affect our happiness and, in the next paragraphs, we will discuss the importance of some of them.

Water

Being dehydrated can affect your mood, your focus, and the functions of your organs. Try to stop drinking water for four or five hours and then drink some; you will notice a positive change in your mood. We forget to drink water, especially in the winter, and we don't realize the reason for us being depressed, sad, stressed, or sleepy. The benefits of drinking a healthy amount of water every day are numerous. Drinking water is very helpful in losing weight because it is a substitute for alcohol and carbonated soft drinks, which include a lot of calories and sugar. Water also decreases our appetite because it keeps us full and sometimes we confuse hunger and thirst. Whenever you feel hungry, drink water and wait ten minutes; if you are still hungry then you are really hungry, not thirsty. Water also makes you look younger by giving you healthy skin. Your eyes become wider and clearer and it helps get rid of the dark circles beneath your eyes.

Water is very powerful in improving our digestion and detoxing our bodies. I was attending a course called "Maximize Your Physical Energy" in which the trainer told us to drink more water during the week; in the following session we told him about the differences that we noticed. My results were unbelievable; I started to consciously drink more water every day, my productivity increased, and my mood got significantly better. Even my colleagues noticed. Try to drink more water for a week and you will notice the difference.

Fruits and Vegetables

Eating fruits and vegetables that contain a decent amount of water, like watermelon and cucumber, are very enjoyable and beneficial if you don't want to drink more water.

According to a study done by Professor Andrew Oswald and Dr. Redzo Mujcic at the University of Warwick, eating fruits and vegetables boost our happiness far quicker than they improve human health.[14] People who added up to eight portions of fruits and vegetables into their daily diets noticed an increase in their level of happiness equivalent to moving from unemployment to employment.

Cooking

In Idea 45, we will talk about how maintaining healthy relationships can make you happier. When we are trying to enhance our relationships with the ones we love, we underestimate cooking, but cooking with our loved ones can be something that greatly enhances our relationships, resulting an increase in happiness.

42. Move Your Body

I KNOW I MENTIONED at the beginning of this book that I would provide you with easy ideas and methods for a happier life but, after researching and studying happiness for a long time, I found it necessary to mention the idea of having your body moving in order to create positive emotions. 78% of those who are extremely happy said they exercise at least three times per week. Vanessa King, the author of the famous book *10 Keys to Happier Living,* said that it is not easy to feel good emotions while you are sitting.[15]

It does not have to be a very intense workout; it could be a twenty-minute walk. I highly recommend yoga because it works on strengthening the body and clearing the mind at the same time. The benefits of physical activity are countless; for example, you have a sense of accomplishment when you practice a physical activity because you get good at it, you lift a higher weight in the gym, you break your own records in running a specific distance, or you can finally make a yoga pose that was challenging for you.

Sandra a yoga teacher from Cairo also recommends yoga as a way to increase happiness. "I started yoga in March 2011," she told me. "It was two months after the revolution. I was living in Vancouver and I had to come back because my mother was in her last stage of cancer. She only had six months to live. I was taking care of her with my sister, aunts, and grandma. It was a hard time because I was just getting into a new career, I was very active, I had a lot of friends, and I went out a lot.

"But when I came back to Cairo I felt like a stranger in my own family. I was out of Egypt for about six years. I did not know what to do with myself and with my time. Initially, I decided to do yoga because a friend of mine in Vancouver recommended it. I was attracted to the physical side of it because I was a gym addict and because my mother was also an athlete. I felt guilty going to the gym while she was sick in bed and unable to move.

"A lot of the time I had to help lift her to the bathroom, so I needed to be present. That's why I ultimately chose yoga; it was discrete and I could do it in the home. I was in my room with my laptop for one hour per day and when we moved my mother to the hospital for three months I took my yoga mat with me and practiced every day. March 2018 marks eight years of an almost daily practice—known as sadhana or commitment—to self through spiritual purification."

The second benefit of exercising is that it reduces insomnia and gives you a deeper sleep. Since you've exerted all the energy your body generated throughout the day, you don't have the energy for late night overthinking, which many people suffer from.

Physical activity can make you more resilient. In a study performed by Stanford University on athletic students, they found physical activity had a number of benefits but the most obvious one was it made them more resilient and helped them cope better with adversity.[16] Personally, whenever I face a challenge or feel depressed, I go for a run or hit the gym; it clears my mind, reduces the pressure of the situation, and gives me a sense of freedom, independence, and power. If you have never practiced sports before, consider trying different things until you find something that suits your lifestyle. I believe that practicing sports is a flexible activity; it could be done alone or with people, in the street, at home or at the gym, during the day or at night, in the winter or in the summer. In order to have this flexibility, you have to learn about different types of exercises that suit various situations and environments. I say this because sports are an instant hack towards happiness; they can change your mood instantly.

43. Increase Your Happiness Hormones

THERE ARE NUMEROUS hormones like serotonin, endorphin, dopamine, and oxytocin that our mind excretes when we are happy. Here are some ways to help boost them:

1. Movement
2. Physical contact (This explains why the couples who hug the most are the happiest.)
3. Meditation
4. Laughter
5. Exposure to natural light
6. Consuming less caffeine
7. Decreasing your sugar intake
8. Listening sincerely to someone

44. Following Your Lusts and Desires Will Not Make You Happy

I DON'T KNOW HOW TO make you believe it, but I insist that following your lusts and desires will make you sad. You will always want more and you will lose your soul in the process. You will also face troubles and debts in order to experience those desires. While studying neuro-linguistic programming, I learned that "whatever solution to a problem that does not serve your wholeness is going to make the situation even worse".[17] For example, if you are trying to forget a problem by taking drugs or drinking alcohol, your behavior will make the situation worse. If you are having troubles with your partner and you decide to cheat on her/him, your behavior will gradually make the situation worse. It is going to bring you temporary joy but results in long-term regret and pain.

Part Four:
Happy Relationships

I n this part, I will share some tips that will help you create nurturing and encouraging relationships and avoid toxic and unhealthy relationships.

45. Maintain Good Relationships

THERE WAS A STUDY DONE by Harvard University that was conducted on the same people for seventy-five years, from the time they were college students until their eighties and nineties. Harvard discovered that the people who were maintaining good and healthy relationships in their fifties were mentally and physically healthier in their eighties and nineties.[18] Sharing love and respect promotes satisfaction and positive self-worth.

This is not a book about relationships, but these are some tips that will help you maintain healthy relationships.

1. Find and maintain relationships with people that have similar values, interests, and hobbies as you because it is easier to maintain healthy relationships with people who you share things in common with.
2. Confront your problems; don't be angry and silent. Tell your partner or friend what makes you feel bad, but at the right time and with elegance, confidence, and respect. Accumulating sadness or anger will negatively affect your relationships in the long term.
3. Be objective, not subjective. Don't hate the person for their mistakes; hate the act that he committed and talk about how you both can make sure it doesn't happen again. Behaviors change over time, so don't attach a person to their behavior.

4. Don't stay in a relationship that doesn't help you evolve. Relationships are not the goal; our evolution throughout a relationship is the goal. Accordingly, don't stay in a relationship just for the sake of being in a relationship.

5. Don't assume you know someone, no matter how long you have been in a relationship with them; there are always some aspects of a person you don't know. In order to get to know a different aspect of a person, ask new questions, experience something new together, or just go somewhere special. You will be amazed by the number of things you didn't know about that person after all your time together. Diversifying your experiences and discussions will help you discover new aspects about that person. This will enhance your relationship with them, as you will get to know all their sides.

Dalia from Egypt used similar tips to get to know her classmates better. This is what she told me: "I used to be grumpy and angry all the time, especially during the latter years of primary school. The kids around me used to ignore me and make fun of my weird pronunciation. In the beginning, I ignored them and kept my anger inside, which made them think I was OK with it, so they continued to unintentionally bully me.

"Later, I started to explode and throw tantrums. In my mind, it was completely justifiable since I tolerated a lot, but in their minds, it was a spontaneous reaction that had no cause behind it. Consequently, we started fighting constantly. In prep school, I was completely drained and all I wanted was to change schools and keep everything behind me. Luckily for me, I didn't change schools right away because I had to finish the academic year, which made me decide that no matter what anyone said or did, I wouldn't lose my temper or fight.

"That decision changed my life because I was able to truly listen to others and see their point of view. Of course, my anger management wasn't perfect until a few years later, but I was glad to see my life improving one step at a time. Now, the people who I used to fight with became my closest friends, even though we rarely saw each other after changing schools. All of this made me realize that happiness was a choice, not an effect of an event or a thing."

By considering the feelings of others around her and taking control of her emotions, Dalia was able to create lifelong friendships and turn enemies into allies.

46. Don't Care About What People Think of You

NO MATTER HOW CLICHÉ it may sound, I have to say it because it's real. People's opinions are variable and inconstant. Consequently, in order to please everyone all the time, you would have to change your behavior consistently, which contradicts Idea 30—to be congruent. It is also impossible. In order to please everyone, you would have to change your behaviors frequently, which is something that would contradict your values, beliefs, or feelings and, consequently, make you unhappy. It is not that people think of us in a certain way; it is our refusal to be the person they think we are. If we were okay with them thinking of us in a certain way, we would feel calm and secure.

On the other hand, don't be extreme about it; don't try to bother people all the time in order to prove to yourself that you don't care what other people think of you; you will end up being hated by most of them. Be true to who you are without requiring validation from anyone. The Sufi culture has the same concept; they say "praise and vilify should become equal to you". Be aware that when you decide to be happy you might look strange to some people. Some people might try to make you feel ridiculous, but that is not you; it is their interpretation of you which reflects who they are, not who you are. What people think of you is a reflection of them, so don't be angry with them. On the contrary, you can be sympathetic to them because they are missing the good feelings that you feel. Don't try to force your ideas on them in order to change them because everyone has their own journey and path.

Theodore Roosevelt, an American author who served as the 26th President of the United States from 1901 to 1909, wrote a quote that really inspired me. I always struggled with people telling me how to live better. They would say, "Who do you think you are?" or "You are not qualified enough to do this." When I read Roosevelt's quote, it all became clear. He said, "It is not the critic who counts; not the man who points out how the strong man stumbles, or where the doer of deeds could have done them better. The credit belongs to the man who is actually in the arena, whose face is marred by dust and sweat and blood; who strives valiantly; who errs, who comes short again and again, because there is no effort without error and shortcoming; but who does actually strive to do the deeds; who knows great enthusiasms, the great devotions; who spends himself in a worthy cause; who at the best knows in the end the triumph of high achievement, and who at the worst, if he fails, at least fails while daring greatly, so that his place shall never be with those cold and timid souls who neither know victory nor defeat."[19]

After reading that quote, I realized there were people who were not doing anything with their lives; instead, they were watching and criticizing other people's lives. Maybe we made them think they had the authority to discourage us. If we really listened to them or behaved according to their advice, we would probably screw up because they don't have the knowledge or the experience that gives them the authority to advise us. It is our insecurities that made them so confident.

There will be three types of people who will show up when you start to do something you love or when you create something new. The first type is the person who tries to shame you. This person will tell you that you are not enough and, when you start to feel confident, they will make you question yourself. The second type is the person who will make you feel small, who will tell you that you are too late, that there are so many other people who are doing it better than you or that what you are doing has no impact. The third type is the person who will compare you to others, telling you about how trained, qualified, or talented they are. Knowing and accepting that these three types of people will show up will make you feel secure and confident when dealing with them. Next time they try to tell you what you should do, remind yourself to respect them but not to listen to them. You have to be careful because these types of people could be the closest people to you; they could even turn out to be you.

47. Don't Compare Yourself to Others

JOHN R. WOODEN, THE legendary basketball player and coach, was the first person to be inducted into the Basketball Hall of Fame as a player and as a coach. He never watched a match of his opponents. He always encouraged his team players to do their best. It has been said that the easiest road to sadness and depression is to compare your life to other people's lives, and it's true. First, you don't know everything about their lives; they may be suffering in different ways or they might not even be doing that well in the field which you're envious of. In our modern age, showing off your "perfect life" is easy with social media platforms and filters, but you have to notice that people are posting the highlights of their lives and you are comparing those highlights to your lesser moments, which is not fair.

Second, everybody has their own path; some might take longer than others to achieve their goals and some might have a better social life than a financial one and vice versa. A study was conducted by the Happiness Research Institute in Denmark that experimented on two groups; one of them was asked not to log into their social media accounts for one week while the other group had normal access to their accounts. At the end of the experiment, they found that the group that had not accessed their social media accounts had achieved a higher level of life satisfaction.[20]

Jack Ma, the owner of Ali Baba Empire, said his biggest regret was not spending more time with his family and children. But at the same time, so many people were envious of him for having so much money. In order to stop comparing ourselves to others, we need to transform our way of thinking from the "me vs. you" mentality into the "us" mentality. We should hope for everybody to succeed in life because that will make our lives much easier. For example, imagine that every employee, police officer, lawyer, and worker was doing very well in life. Every product and service you use or consume would have a world-class quality.

If you insist on comparing yourself to others, then compare in order to be inspired by how much you can achieve. See what the world is missing and try to fill it; turn it into a learning experience.

48. Surround Yourself with People Who Share Your Mission

HAPPINESS IS A SOCIAL emotion. If you are walking alone with a big smile on your face, you are going to look ridiculous, but if there is someone walking with you, it will look normal. If you are smiling at a stranger, you are giving him a sign that he can approach you. I was attending a sermon where the imam talked about how we could be better Muslims and he gave us an example that I will never forget. He told us that if we put a carrot in honey, it will be a jam but if we put it in salt, it will be a pickle. This also applies to us as human beings; we are what we are because of our surroundings. I know that having the will to defeat our surroundings and become something else seems hard, but it will be worth it.

After hearing that example, I thought about what I want in my life. I realized that if I want to achieve something I should surround myself with the things that will help me achieve it; these surroundings could be people who have the same goals as me or a society that supports my ideas and helps me grow.

Lily from Mexico felt similarly. "Being part of a meditation group helped me focus on and pursue my goals," she commented. Having a group of like-minded individuals to talk with helps us grow and find happiness.

Here is another example: I wanted to become fit and athletic, so I started to subscribe to channels on YouTube that post videos on training and nutrition. I went to the gym and tried to make some friends there. I wanted to be mindful and calm, so I went to yoga and meditation classes and I followed some yogis on Facebook and other online platforms. I wanted to be happy, so I started to read every book that talked about happiness. I started to support every happy action that comes my way and then I finally started to study and write about happiness.

You too can monitor the people around you who seem happy and try to get closer to them. Reality is relative from one person to another and if you surround yourself with happy people you will create a happier reality.

49. Ask Positive Questions

ASKING QUESTIONS IS considered a very powerful method to control our focus, so in order to focus on being happy, we have to ask ourselves and the people around us positive questions, questions that shift our focus and theirs. Life coaches and therapists are using these questions to let their clients find the answers by themselves; our subconscious creates answers and solutions, but we just have to ask the right questions in order to compel it to focus on happiness. Here are some questions that can shift your focus to happiness. You can also create or search for more.

1. What do you love the most about your city?
2. What is your happiest memory?
3. What is the best thing that happened to you today?
4. What is the best compliment that you have ever received?
5. What makes your soul sing?
6. Where is your happy place?
7. How old would you be if you didn't know how old you were?
8. What are you most grateful for?
9. If joy became the national currency, what kind of work would make you wealthy?
10. What do you love the most about your mother/son/best friend (any person whom you love)?
11. What are the changes in your personality that you are most proud of?
12. What excites you about the future?
13. How can you make yourself happy?
14. Who has had the most positive impact on your life?
15. Who do you love and why do you love them?
16. What comes easily to you in life?
17. How can you help someone today?
18. How many times did you make someone laugh?

After asking yourself these questions, you will notice your mood has lightened. Commit to asking yourself one positive question every day.

50. In a World Full of Red Buttons, Be a Green One

IN A TED TALK CALLED "Is the Glass Half Full or Half Empty? The Final Proof!" Leo Bormans, the writer of the bestseller *The World Book of Happiness*, said that society is divided into two kinds of buttons: the red buttons, which represent the pessimists, and the green buttons, which are the optimists.[21] The red buttons can be identified very quickly because they are always talking about themselves, their past, and their problems. The green buttons, on the other hand, are the ones who are talking about we, us, the future, solutions, and the good things happening around them. Whether you are a green button or a red button, your attitude is contagious; you are spreading what you share and talk about. You are the person that hears you the most, so be careful what you talk about because you are listening.

51. Don't Let Anyone Pull You to His/Her Energy

WHENEVER SOMEONE IS angry at you, don't let them pull you into their energy or state; try to protect your peace and calmness by knowing that they are only harming themselves. Be aware of your own values and manners and stick to them. For example, I used to ignore the people who offended me; I used to feel sorry for myself for not responding and I decided to change that by responding to anyone that tries to offend me, but by doing that I found myself feeling guilty and worse because it was not me. It was something that went against the values and manners I believed in. I stopped responding to people who insult me, knowing that it would make me feel worse and it would not make me any better than them.

I watched an interview with a very successful Egyptian singer and the interviewer asked him, "Why don't you respond to all the insults that people address to you?" The singer said, "I will not let someone pull me to his energy by insult and bad behavior. On the contrary, I will pull him to my energy with forgiveness and good manners." That is how we make a better world.

There is a very powerful exercise I learned from Deepak Chopra, an American author, and public speaker. The exercise helped me a lot in maintaining my inner peace and calmness when someone was behaving in an unpleasant way towards me; I separated or isolated myself from the situation by noticing where in my body I felt the emotion. Then I asked myself, "If I were someone else, what advice would I give to myself? How would I advise myself to behave in this situation?" It may not be an easy thing to do at the beginning, but by practicing it and by finding out how much energy you will save and how peaceful you will feel afterward, it will become easy and enjoyable.

52. Happiness Sells

WHY DOES COCA-COLA include the word happiness in almost every commercial they make? Think of any advertisement you have watched; you won't be able to recall one that shows a sad person who consumes the product or the service which the advertiser is wishing to sell. They want the audience to link happiness to their products and/or services. So why don't we do the same? Why don't we make people link happiness and cheerfulness to us? Not by faking happiness, but by making it. This concept has a lot of benefits. People love to work with happy people; they want to buy from them, help them, get married to them, and be around them. Being happy will give you an advantage over your competitors, no matter what field you are in.

Part Five:
Interviews with People Who Finished the 100 Happy Days Challenge

T

he 100 Happy Days Challenge is an initiative founded by Dmitry Golubnichy, a Ukrainian young man living in Zurich, Switzerland. When I listened to why he started the challenge, I found his reasoning was similar to my reasoning behind writing this book. He had done a lot of things that seemed to make everyone happy, but it didn't make him happy. You can find out more about the challenge onhttp://100happydays.com/.

These interviews were provided by people around the world who completed the 100 Happy Days Challenge. From these interviews, I gathered that you find happiness by looking for it and that happiness can be found in the simplest things.

Azza:

WHAT MADE YOU START this challenge?

I always wondered what the true meaning of happiness was. I had to dig for it and it was definitely worth the try. I started googling what happiness was and boom! I found this challenge. I registered without thinking.

What was the most enjoyable thing about it?

It made me see beyond the surface. I started understanding the meaning of the proverb "happiness comes from the smallest things" and I started waking up every day, thinking about what was going to make me happy that day, so I could complete my challenge... which was fun.

What was the most challenging thing about it?

When I couldn't find something that made me happy and I had to go through my whole day to have a closer look at happiness.

What are the myths that you discovered about happiness?

The biggest myth was that happiness comes from the outside: the circumstances, events, or people around us. That was the biggest lie. I realized thereafter that happiness comes from within. It is generated from the inside out.

What changed in your life after finishing it?

My whole perspective on life has changed, as well as my daily activities and the way I utilize my energy. I started meditating, I became very picky about who I hang out with, and I realized how lucky I am.

What did other people notice about you during and after finishing the challenge?

The close ones noticed that I'd changed drastically. I became more of a carefree and wiser person. That's what they said.

What would you say to people to encourage them to start the challenge?

What are you going to lose if you accept the challenge? For me, my whole life changed with a mouse click when I decided to register for the 100 Happy Days Challenge. Always have the guts to be happy.

Ghada

WHAT MADE YOU START this challenge?

One of my friends started it and advised me to start it with her.

What was the most enjoyable thing about it?

I discovered that the little things make me happy more than the big things. Also, I noticed some details in my life that I wasn't seeing.

What was the most challenging thing about it?

Mm, it takes a lot of time. I started on the 7th of November 2014 and I finished on the 21st of February 2016.

What are the myths that you discovered about happiness?

I was hearing the same saying every day: You are a strong woman! All your days are happy! Why?! How? They didn't understand the meaning of happiness, unfortunately. You can feel happiness only if you decide to. You are responsible for your happiness.

What changed in your life after finishing it?

I can look at things as a way to be happy. I can create happiness from the little things.

What did other people notice about you during and after finishing the challenge?

They were very happy when I shared my happy days with them.

What would you say to people to encourage them to start the challenge?

You should try it! I'm sure you will be one of the happiest people in the world.

Meital

WHAT MADE YOU START this challenge?

I read about this challenge a while ago and I wanted to try it but chose to wait for a special date to start or end it. Then I decided to count to 100 days before my birthday so that the challenge would have a perfect end date.

What was the most enjoyable thing about it?

Not too long after I started, it became clear to me that the little things that make you happy have been there every day and they don't have to be planned or anything. A good cup of coffee or a nice sunset view can make your day if you just pay attention.

What was the most challenging thing about it?

Every person has a bad day, some are just worse than others. It could be difficult to find happiness on days like those, but the search for happiness could help you snap out of your mood.

What are the myths that you discovered about happiness?

I discovered that you need to do so many things in order to be happy, things that are not part of your daily routine. But the first time I saw the amazing sunset was when I realized that happiness was everywhere.

What changed in your life after finishing it?

I started noticing more of the little things and moments that make me happy daily.

What did other people notice about you during and after finishing the challenge?

They noticed that I'd learned to be happier with daily moments. I was always a happy person, but sometimes I broke down and let my negative thoughts control me. Now I try to look more for the good things, even on bad days.

What would you say to people to encourage them to start the challenge?

If you took this challenge seriously, it would help you remember that happiness does exist, everywhere and every day. You just have to keep your eyes and mind wide open so that it can make you stronger and happier.

Esraa

WHAT MADE YOU START this challenge?

One of my friends was doing the challenge and it made me want to try it. I wanted to challenge myself, to make myself happy, and to try new things.

What was the most enjoyable thing about it?

The most enjoyable thing was that people started to check in on me and ask me about my progress. They asked questions like, "What is the challenge of the day?"

What was the most challenging thing about it?

The most challenging thing was going through bad days, when you cannot even smile due to the problems that you face throughout the day. But as a helping tip, I would buy a gift for a friend or I would invite one out, thinking that if I cannot make myself happy, then I can help cheer up someone else and maybe happiness will be transferred to me.

What are the myths that you discovered about happiness?

It is more of a belief than a discovery. I believed that happiness was a decision. Whoever wants to be happy could be happy. There are a million things that happen to us which can make us happy, but we don't see them because we are not conscious. Happiness is very simple.

What changed in your life after finishing it?

I began to love myself and take care of me.

What did other people notice about you during and after finishing the challenge?

People noticed that I was really happy during this challenge and that I learned a lot of things.

What would you say to people to encourage them to start the challenge?

The challenge is important because it makes you focus on the things that make you feel happy throughout the day and neglect the things that bother you. It makes you learn new things. It teaches you that you shouldn't lose yourself in work or study. Having done this challenge, I learned Arabic calligraphy, embroidery, crochet, charcoal drawing, and pastel colors. I saw a lot of movies, read a lot of books, and I made myself and my friends happy.

Dalia

WHAT MADE YOU START this challenge?

It was the third time that I had started the challenge. The first time was in 2015 but I didn't finish it because I was not okay. But for the third time, I finished it. I started it because it was something new and cheerful, so I said, "Why not?" In 2016, I started it because of the encouragement of a friend. He was hoping that I could achieve a better state and finish it. In 2017, I started it because of a group called "Losers Hub". It encouraged people to try new things, no matter the outcome.

What was the most enjoyable thing about it?

The most enjoyable thing was that every day I was searching for something new. This made me happy. It made me enjoy my days by appreciating the good things that happen throughout each day. During the second trial in 2016, I was trying to search for the things that made me feel happy, no matter how small they were. I was trying to appreciate the smallest positive thing that happened each day.

What was the most challenging thing about it?

The most challenging thing was that I might have to do certain things to be happy, but after a while I started to appreciate what I had done in order to feel like I achieved something.

What are the myths that you discovered about happiness?

I discovered that happiness is a journey, not a destination. With every day and every step I take, I find out that happiness is in the actions I take, not the outcome I get.

What changed in your life after finishing it?

After finishing the 100 Happy Days Challenge, I discovered that I had achieved something and that my level of happiness went from minus to six or seven up of ten. I met new people, I developed the habit of happiness, and I started to be happy as much as I could.

What did other people notice about you during and after finishing the challenge?

During the challenge, I was posting my progress on Facebook and I didn't imagine that people would follow my progress. After a while, I discovered that people were following me, and that motivated me. They told me that I inspired them and that I made them believe that happiness does exist.

What would you say to people to encourage them to start the challenge?

If I had to say something to motivate people to start this challenge, I would say that happiness is a decision. Just decide, even if you don't know it is about building a habit. The more you do it, the more you will get used to it.

I will be very grateful and appreciative if you can leave a review, it helps me spread the message of happiness.

Citations

ALCOTT, LOUISA MAY. "15 Tips from Famous Authors to Help You Finally Write That Novel." *Mental Floss,*
  https://mentalfloss.com/article/88662/
15-tips-famous-authors-help-you-finally-write-novel
  Merriam-Webster's Online Dictionary. "Happiness."
  https://www.merriam-webster.com/dictionary/happiness
  Prentice, Kelly. "There is No App for Happiness: An Interview with Max Strom." *Elephant Journal,* 2013.
  Kubansky, Laura. "The Biology of Emotion—and What It May Teach Us About Helping People to Live Longer." Harvard University: Center on the Developing Child, March 1, 2010, https://www.hsph.harvard.edu/news/magazine/happiness-stress-heart-disease/
  "Human Brain—Neuroscience—Cognitive Science." *Basic Knowledge 101,* http://www.basicknowledge101.com/subjects/brain.html
  Neff, Kristin. *Self-Compassion: The Proven Power of Being Kind to Yourself.* William Morrow Paperbacks, 2015.
  Ben-Shahar, Tal. "Positive Psychology: The Science of Happiness." *YouTube,* April 29, 2014, https://www.youtube.com/watch?v=KB8Usl6aX2I
  Mother Teresa. "Anti-war Quote." *Goodreads,* https://www.goodreads.com/quotes/690241-i-was-once-asked-why-i-don-t-participate-in-anti-war
  Esrock, Robin. *Learn to Travel — Travel to Learn.* TEDx, 2013, https://ed.ted.com/on/9Imcch6g
  Canfield, Jack. *The Success Principles: How to Get from Where You Are to Where You Want to Be.* William Morrow Paperbacks, 2006.
  Mays, Benjamin E. "Benjamin E. Mays on Setting Goals and the Importance of Having Them." Lawtology, November 1, 2016, https://lawtology.com/benjamin-e-mays-setting-goals-importance[1]

Cuddy, Amy. *Your Body Language May Shape Who You Are*. TED, 2012, https://www.ted.com/talks/ amy_cuddy_your_body_language_shapes_who_you_are

Fields Wilburn, Joshua. *Minimalism: Live a Meaningful Life*. Asymmetrical Press, 2011.

Virgin, J.J. *The Virgin Diet*. William Morrow Paperbacks, 2015.

Mujcic, Redzo and Oswald, Andrew. "Evolution of Well-Being and Happiness After Increases in Consumption of Fruits and Vegetables." *American Journal of Public Health,* 2016.

King, Vanessa. *10 Keys to Happier Living*. Headline, 2017.

Trudeau and Shephard. "Physical Education, School Physical Activity, School Sports and Academic Performance." *International Journal of Behavioral Nutrition and Physical Activity*, 2008.

The International Federation for Coaching and NLP. "Neuro-linguistic Programming Practitioner Materials."

Mineo, Liz. "Good genes are nice, but joy is better." *The Harvard Gazette,* 2017.

Brown, Brené. *Daring Greatly: How the Courage to Be Vulnerable Transforms the Way We Live, Love, Parent, and Lead*. Avery, 2015.

The Happiness Research Institute. *The Facebook Experiment*. The Happiness Research Institute, Denmark, 2015.

Bormans, Leo. *Is the Glass Half Empty or Half Full? The Final Proof!* TEDx, 2012, https://www.youtube.com/watch?v=oPBC15XYl3Q

---

1.   https://lawtology.com/benjamin-e-mays-setting-goals-importance/

[1] Alcott, Louisa May. "15 Tips from Famous Authors to Help You Finally Write That Novel." *Mental Floss,* https://mentalfloss.com/article/88662/15-tips-famous-authors-help-you-finally-write-novel

[2] Merriam-Webster's Online Dictionary. "Happiness." https://www.merriam-webster.com/dictionary/happiness

[3] Prentice, Kelly. "There is No App for Happiness: An Interview with Max Strom." *Elephant Journal,* 2013.

[4] Kubansky, Laura. "The Biology of Emotion—and What It May Teach Us About Helping People to Live Longer." Harvard University: Center on the Developing Child, March 1, 2010, https://www.hsph.harvard.edu/news/magazine/happiness-stress-heart-disease/

[5] "Human Brain—Neuroscience—Cognitive Science." *Basic Knowledge 101,* http://www.basicknowledge101.com/subjects/brain.html

[6] Neff, Kristin. *Self-Compassion: The Proven Power of Being Kind to Yourself.* William Morrow Paperbacks, 2015.

[7] Ben-Shahar, Tal. "Positive Psychology: The Science of Happiness." *YouTube,* April 29, 2014, https://www.youtube.com/watch?v=KB8Usl6aX2I

[8] Mother Teresa. "Anti-war Quote." *Goodreads,* https://www.goodreads.com/quotes/690241-i-was-once-asked-why-i-don-t-participate-in-anti-war

[9] Esrock, Robin. *Learn to Travel — Travel to Learn.* TEDx, 2013, https://ed.ted.com/on/9Imcch6g

[10] Canfield, Jack. *The Success Principles: How to Get from Where You Are to Where You Want to Be.* William Morrow Paperbacks, 2006.

[11] Mays, Benjamin E. "Benjamin E. Mays on Setting Goals and the Importance of Having Them." Lawtology, November 1, 2016, https://lawtology.com/benjamin-e-mays-setting-goals-importance/

[12] Cuddy, Amy. *Your Body Language May Shape Who You Are.* TED, 2012, https://www.ted.com/talks/amy_cuddy_your_body_language_shapes_who_you_are

[13] Fields Wilburn, Joshua. *Minimalism: Live a Meaningful Life.* Asymmetrical Press, 2011.

[14] Mujcic, Redzo and Oswald, Andrew. "Evolution of Well-Being and Happiness After Increases in Consumption of Fruits and Vegetables." *American Journal of Public Health,* 2016.

[15] King, Vanessa. *10 Keys to Happier Living.* Headline, 2017.

[16] Trudeau and Shephard. "Physical Education, School Physical Activity, School Sports and Academic Performance." *International Journal of Behavioral Nutrition and Physical Activity,* 2008.

[17] The International Federation for Coaching and NLP. "Neuro-linguistic Programming Practitioner Materials."

[18] Mineo, Liz. "Good genes are nice, but joy is better." *The Harvard Gazette,* 2017.

[19] Brown, Brené. *Daring Greatly: How the Courage to Be Vulnerable Transforms the Way We Live, Love, Parent, and Lead.* Avery, 2015.

[20] The Happiness Research Institute. *The Facebook Experiment.* The Happiness Research Institute, Denmark, 2015.

[21] Bormans, Leo. *Is the Glass Half Empty or Half Full? The Final Proof!* TEDx, 2012, https://www.youtube.com/watch?v=oPBC15XYl3Q

About the Author

I am a best selling author and a judge in the family court since 2009, but I have been following my passion for self-help and spirituality since 2005. I am a certified NLP practitioner by the international federation of coaching, NLP and Time Line therapy practitioner by the TimeLine therapy association, and author of the book "The forgotten art of happiness". I attended a numerous seminars and workshops online and offline on coaching, meditation, spirituality, and business. My exposure to the domestic conflicts in the family court put me close to real life scenarios, I have seen the truth of human emotions and how feelings can change our decisions and my passion took me from a shy anxious thin guy to a fit, self-aware, determined man. I went through a long journey of self-discovery by consuming a lot of knowledge, writing, and monitoring and analyzing my actions. I am also the founder of A Space to Be; it is an initiative which organizes workshops, group discussions, and retreats to help people find out who they really are.